Bimini Glass and the Politics of Survival

Angela M Bowey and Raymond F. Berger

Bimini Glass

CONTENTS

ACKNOWLEDGMENTS

This book has taken many years to complete. Thank you Raymond, my co-author, for your patience and all your help.

The photographs in this book are from four different collections, the collection inherited by Raymond Berger from his father Josef Berger and his uncle Fritz Lampl, the very extensive collection built up by Pipin Henzl in Vienna, the collection inherited by Sebastian Gomperts in London from his mother Barbara Gomperts a friend of Fritz Lampl, and the collection in the archives of the MAK museum in Vienna. Sincere thanks to the people who kindly allowed us to photograph their collections for this book.

Thanks also to Gail Bardhan and the Corning Museum of Glass Rakow Library for source information and advice. And to Anne Nichols who helped considerably with research on the companies and the people involved.

Thanks to Michael Bowey for taking photographs, recording our interviews, and editing the text. You were a real help. And to Jane Bailey for proof editing the text, thank you so much.

To Ann Berger for her patience and kindness through this long gestation period, our sincere thanks

1: BIMINI GLASS – THE STORY

The Politics of Hate

This is the story of a family of young artists who lived and trained in Vienna and became world famous for their contributions to the arts in the 1920s and 30s. The politics of hate were surging around Europe in those years, with Jews, gypsies, communists and others being blamed for the privations, shortages and inequalities that were causing widespread misery amongst some people. Germany was an unhappy country, smarting from the harsh penalties imposed by the Allies after the 1st World War. Adolf Hitler stirred up hatred and swept into power first in Germany and then with her allies.

The consequences were enormous, with millions of people being "exterminated" in the name of "ethnic cleansing", and millions of others dying in the war which ensued. This world-scale tragedy has been written about many times, and we are only touching on a small part of that history here. For the people who survived those years there were tragedies in their lives caused by the hatred they faced and triumphs when they found solutions to their hardships.

We cast light on one small mosaic in a huge kaleidoscope of human endeavour - the survival of a peer group of artists who set up the Bimini Glass Werkstatte (workshop) in Vienna in the 1920s and so created a legend. Their legacy includes Bimini Glass and the generic flood of Bimini-style glass popular with collectors across the world today.

Fritz Lampl, Josef, Artur, Hilde and Fritzi Berger, along with Margarete Hamerschlag

Fritz Lampl was a poet and writer who turned to designing art glass, his wife Hilde and her sister Fritzi (Fredericke) were haute couture dress designers, their brothers Josef and Artur Berger were architects and designers, and Josef's wife Margarete was a painter, illustrator and writer. They all became involved in designing glass for the Bimini workshop and helping to promote it. Each exhibited their work around the world and won prestigious international prizes, but being from Jewish families they had to flee from Vienna when Nazi Germany annexed Austria in the 1930s. The group left behind their workshops, their homes, and the stocks of their creations.

Artur fled to Russia and became Art Director for the State film company Mosfilm. Fritzi (Hilde's sister) went to the USA to continue her haute couture career. The other four, Fritz Lampl and Hilde, Josef Berger and Margarete, eventually settled in war-time London and started from scratch to re-establish their studios and their lives. This is their story.

Vienna in the 1920s

The story begins in the city of Vienna just after the First World War. Capital of the huge Austro-Hungarian Empire before that war, Vienna played a major role in the art and politics of Europe at the time. They declared war on Serbia in July 1914, effectively starting WW1. Austria fared very badly during that war, and when defeat was unavoidable the Emperor, Kaiser Charles I abdicated and the country became a republic (November 1918). By then the Bank of Vienna had collapsed, inflation was growing out of control, and thousands of Viennese who had invested their savings in war bonds now found them worthless. The Allies drawing up the Treaty of Versailles at the Paris Peace Conference in June of 1919 decided that Austria was "so impoverished" she could not pay reparations to the Allies as other countries, mainly Germany, were required to do. Instead they handed over precious resources such as timber, ore and livestock to the Allied countries, and to some extent paid for property that had been illegally seized.

Out of this political and economic chaos a new Vienna emerged. Elections were held in May 1919 with all citizens having equal rights to vote, men and women, rich and poor and all religious and ethnic groups. This was years before other developed countries awarded such universal rights. The left wing Social Democratic Party won a clear majority in the election and Red Vienna became the popular name for the capital of Austria.

Red Vienna's new government had many problems to deal with. The population of the city had swelled with refugees from other parts of Europe and returning soldiers who were looking for work and places to live. There was overcrowding, illness (especially Spanish flu), poverty, and a lack of work. The new boundaries drawn up at the Treaty of Versailles now left Austria with a mere eighth of the lands and people it had previously governed. This meant that supplies of food and raw materials into the capital city were scarce. There was however no shortage of brilliant people fired by enthusiasm and hunger for the new regime and the "modernization" of Vienna.

Writing in 1944 Karl Polanyi said: "Vienna achieved one of the most spectacular cultural triumphs of Western history … a rise in the condition of a highly developed industrial working class which, protected by the Vienna system, withstood the degrading effects of grave economic dislocation and achieved a level never reached before by the masses of the people in any industrial society." (Polanyi. p. 298)*.

Amongst the far-reaching changes that were introduced were the eight hour working day, an unemployment benefit payment system, and an extensive state-subsidised building programme for public housing projects. The rents for these flats were kept affordable for workers. There were mother and baby benefits, free medical services, facilities for child care to enable mothers to return to work, sports facilities and public baths. Such advances were not to be seen in other European or Western Societies for decades to come. All this public expenditure was funded from new taxes, from Federal funds, and from investments. Initial enthusiasm for the socialist programme faded over the years amongst the affluent, conservative, supporters of the opposition Christian Social Party.

Books and texts referred to in this chapter are listed alphabetically at the end of the book.

Culture and Art in Vienna

Through these turbulent times, Vienna maintained its place as a major artistic and cultural centre. Artists, philosophers, the "intelligentsia" in all fields, were attracted to Vienna as exiles or chose to join the dynamic progressive Viennese culture. Amongst the many memorable names living in Vienna at that time were Sigmund Freud, Alfred Adler, Ludwig Wittgenstein, Adolf Loos, Oskar Kokoschka, Richard Strauss, Fritz Kriesler, Gustav Klimt, Koloman Moser and Josef Hoffmann. Giants in their fields, they found in Vienna a fertile culture where their influence and ideas could flourish.

From the late 19th century Viennese coffee houses played an important part in shaping Viennese culture. The "Viennese Coffee House Culture" is listed as "Intangible Cultural Heritage" in the UNESCO inventory of such institutions. The typical Viennese Coffee Houses sold an excellent variety of coffee plus snacks, and provided international newspapers for their customers to read. Their interior design was typically Historismus style with marble table tops, bentwood chairs and tables for newspapers. The Austrian writer Stefan Zweig described the Viennese Coffee House as "actually a sort of democratic club, open to everyone for the price of a cheap cup of coffee, where every guest can sit for hours with this little offering, to talk, write, play cards, receive post, and above all consume an unlimited number of newspapers and journals." He described one such Coffee House, the Café Griensteidl, as the "headquarters of young literature".

Our peer group of young artists were all growing up and training for their professions at this time. Vienna was then a wonderful, carefree, happy society, a city of theatres, concerts, opera, fashionable balls, coffee house cliques of intelligentsia and artists. They took it for granted that their freedom, equality and security would continue indefinitely. They were aware of the troubles in neighbouring countries but most believed that Vienna was safe from them. Kaiser Franz Joseph had ruled the empire for 68 years, contributing to a sense of security and continuity. When his nephew Charles succeeded him in 1916 it was assumed that the stability would continue. Austrian politicians were particularly anxious to ensure that there was no repeat of the Bolshevik Revolution in their country, and no submission to the bullying tactics of the fascists in nearby Germany.

These were the years when the Weiner Werkstatte - Vienna Workshop reached the peak of its popularity. Founded in 1903 by Koloman Moser and Josef Hoffmann, the aim was to modernize the applied arts. With financial support from the industrialist Fritz Wärndorfer, they were able to set up artistic production in three small rooms. Within two years they had grown to a hundred employees working in a three-story building. Designers, artists and architects created designs and master craftsmen produced the "arts and crafts" output in a wide range of craft media. To this day the Wiener Werkstatte is recognised as the pioneer of modern design, and its influence can be seen in such later styles as Bauhaus and Art Deco. Their products were stamped with the WW trademark, shown below, as well as the identity of the designer and that of the craftsman.

Bimini Glass

Charismatic, inspiring teachers were part of that movement and they gave their students a sound understanding of Modern design principles. Our peer group of artists were trained by leading figures from the Wiener Werkstatte, and contributed as designers and artists themselves. Josef and Artur Berger designed apartment blocks of workers flats as recorded on this plaque from the wall of one such building still in use today. Josef's son Raymond and Artur's son Sasha are standing by the plaque on a visit in 2014 to attend the premier of a film about Artur Berger entitled "Journey into a Fog" (the same title as a book by Raymond's mother Margarete).

Some of Josef and Artur's smaller design projects can be found illustrated in books about the Wiener Werkstatte. Fritzi and Hilde Berger were skilled ladies fashion designers. Fritzi illustrated four postcards of her designs in the WW postcard series. Margarete Hamerschlag designed woodcuts and lithographs for books published by the Wiener Werkstatte.

The Bimini Workshop Team

In 1923 the Bimini Glass workshop was founded. At this time the Wiener Werkstatte was starting to decline and they were bankrupt by 1932. "Red Vienna" had been taken over by more conservative politicians and Bimini glass was something completely new. It was eagerly bought by art collectors, stocked in major stores and very swiftly recognized internationally.

Bimini was the brain-child of Fritz Lampl and was brought to life by his peer group of relatives. Fritz was born to an affluent Jewish family in Vienna, Austria in 1892 and raised in a suburb of that city where there was a large Jewish population. His father was a prosperous corn merchant and a civic councilor, a small dry man, very conscious of his rank, whilst Fritz's mother was rather tiny, thin and considered quite authoritarian. Frutz had two elder brothers, August who became an architect, and Paul who chose banking.

In his early years Fritz became a poet and a writer, with poems published in a leading literary review The Brenner and short stories published by a German publisher Jakob Hegner. He suffered with ear problems throughout his youth, and his long periods of recuperation saw him continuing to study philosophy, art, and history as well as literature. He was well-liked amongst his many artist friends who used to meet in the Café Central in Vienna. His sense of humour, wide knowledge and gentle modesty were mentioned many times by his friends.

Fritz was 22 in 1914 when the First World War broke out in Europe, with Germany and Austria fighting against Britain, France and their allies. His two brothers were killed in that war. Fritz's poor health kept him out of the army but he still had to contribute to the war effort and was assigned to the Kreigspressequartier writing propaganda material.

During the war Fritz and his writer and artist friends continued to meet, now in the Cafe Herrenhof. After the war a group of these writers, led by Fritz with Albert Ehrenstein and including Fritz Werfel, formed a writers' cooperative which published a small number of volumes, including Fritz's comedy The Flight, about two young people fleeing from unwelcome constraints. However they failed to convince their more illustrious writer friends to change from their existing publishers, and the publishing venture failed to make a profit. Fritz did not even receive his salary.

It was at the Café Herrenhof that his friends Josef and Artur Berger introduced Fritz to their beautiful sister Hilde. He was entranced by Hilde's gentle beauty and intelligent conversation. When the war ended they were married in a quiet civil ceremony with just a few friends present. Fritz then took his new bride home to tell his parents. His mother in particular had been hoping for a huge family wedding, appropriate for the only surviving son of a rich Jewish family. His parents were furious but Fritz was unmoved by their complaints.

Fritz and Hilde Lampl were close friends with Hilde's sister Fritzi as well as her two brothers. And when brother Josef married Margarete Hamerschlag in 1922 this brought a sixth artist into the family group. Hilde and Fritz, Josef and Margarete were to remain friends for the rest of their lives. The picture below shows two happy teenagers, Margarete (on the right) with her sister Nelly taken about 1914 in Vienna.

Margarete had been born in Vienna in 1902 and from her early childhood she wanted to be an artist. Her mother was so keen to discourage Margarete's desire to learn art that she sent some of her drawings to Koloman Moser, with a letter asking for advice. Many years later Margarete recorded her mother's letter in her own memoirs:

"My daughter, aged seven, doesn't seem interested in anything else but in painting. I enclose some of her work so that you could judge whether there is any sense in letting her go on, or whether my husband and I should rather try to turn her interest onto some field in which she can really succeed".

The opinion of this leading Viennese artist was that Margarete had real talent and "it would be a sin to forbid her to paint" rather that she should be encouraged. And a delighted Margarete was sent to the Junior Art Class when she was only 7, having passed the entrance examination for Franz Cizek's specialist art classes. From the age of 14 and continuing through her teenage years she studied at the Kunstgeverbeschule, the School of Applied Arts under several leading artists and designers of the time. She became a very successful artist and writer, and during her time in Vienna undertook some impressive commissions. Her woodcuts illustrated Edgar Allan Poe's book Die Maske des roten Todes, (Vienna 1924) as well as her own books Kinderfreuden (Vienna 1921) and Die Stadt (Vienna 1923).

All six of our young artists had benefitted from the forward-looking gymnasium education system of the Austro-Hungarian empire and training in the arts provided by the Technical Institutes of Vienna. They were part of the prevailing artistic movements in their city, and spent their evenings enjoying the company of fellow-artists.

Josef Berger was the youngest of the four Berger children, born in 1898 to Pauline and Simon Berger, a clerk in the civil service. Both brothers were conscripted into the Austro-Hungarian army but in 1917 Josef was wounded in Italy and sent home. He then became a student at the Technische Hochschule in Vienna, training in architecture under Adolf Loos and in design with Oskar Strnad, both of them brilliant and charismatic. Under Loos's influence Josef became an advocate of the Modern Movement in architecture and design, characterized by simple lines without superfluous decoration. His elder brother Artur had also trained in architecture and design at the same college under Josef Hoffman and on graduating the younger Berger joined his brother and Martin Ziegler in their architectural practice. They designed Modernist residences for workers, commissioned by the left wing Viennese authorities. Josef also designed Modernist furniture and as the political situation changed in Vienna this became a more important focus of specialism. The picture below shows Josef and Margarete Berger on holiday in Austria.

Joseph's brother Artur was six years his elder, and he too moved away from architecture in the 1920s. The political scene was changing and commissions for workers residences grew scarce. Moving into the design of scenery he designed film sets for epic films directed by Alexander Korda and Michael Curtiz, and the scenery and buildings for a hugely successful film directed by Gustav Ucicky. In 1931 he collaborated with Siegfried Bernfeld on the screenplay for the first film ever directed by Otto Preminger. His success continued into the 1930s but by 1936 the spread of the Austrian Fascist movement and influence in Austria from the Nazi government in Germany had led to people of Jewish origin being banned from working in the film industry in Austria.

Artur left Vienna and made his way north, settling in Russia, where his film industry skills were put to good use by the State film producers Mosfilm. He was the designer for over 50 films during a long career as Art Director of Mosfilm, and his films were watched by some 95 million people in the USSR and her satellite countries. In Moscow he was known by the name Artur Semyonovich Berger and in 1968 was recognized by the Soviet State for his work. He received an award: Meritorious Artist of the Russian Soviet Federative Socialist Republic. He died in retirement in Russia in 1981. Since then there have been festivals of his films held in both Austria and Russia. His nephew, Raymond Berger (co-author of this book) was invited and attended a film festival in Vienna in 2014 which included the premiere showing of the film "Journey into a Fog" about Artur Berger.

Meantime, back in Vienna in the 1920s, the Berger sisters built up a very successful haute couture business. They had a shop in a smart part of Vienna and when Fritzi Berger emigrated to the US in the mid-1930s she was able to continue her successful career in dress design. The four postcards in the Wiener Werkstatte postcard series of designs by Fritzi Berger are shown on the website www.theviennasecession.com and also in the collection at the New York Metropolitan Museum of Art. They are now very collectable. The pictures below show three of the Fritzi Berger designs from postcards numbered 788, 764, and 767 in the W W series.

Bimini Glass

The Bimini Workshop

In 1922 a catastrophic investment by Fritz Lampl's father ruined the Lampl family financially. Both parents died shortly afterwards and this left Fritz with no money and a new wife to support. He was not making enough as a writer.

Seeking a new direction for his career, Fritz Lampl found himself inspired by the fantasy shapes in glass which he saw at an exhibition in Berlin of blown glass figures by Marianne von Allesch. He described these as "poetry materialized" and "frozen poetry". As a young boy he had been fascinated by the itinerant glass blowers who made animals out of hot glass at country fairs, using pedal-powered flames. The Allesch exhibition showed him that flame-worked glass could become serious art, and inspired him to want to create in blown glass himself. He returned from Berlin in 1923 full of enthusiasm and set about his new business, very rapidly achieving undreamed-of success. He rented a basement, recruited an out-of- work industrial glassblower, and called on his brother-in-law's skills as a designer. Josef Berger sat with the glass-blower, drawing pictures of the objects he wanted him to make and discussing the general design, making comments as the design became converted from an idea on paper into a beautiful creation in glass. The team worked with glass tubes of different diameters and colors, some striped. Josef Berger described their work as follows:

First a mouthpiece was formed and then the man suddenly turned up the burner until the glass grew red hot and pliable, expanding as he blew into it, twisting, reheating, and finally cutting the bubble with a knife to form a foot; a vase had been born. There was great virtuosity in handling such brittle material, like taming an obstinate animal. It had to be married to sensitivity to turn craft into art. We learned quickly from each other and soon fantastic animals, vases and figures emerged, which the glass blower then multiplied on his own.

Artur Berger was called into the project and more glass-blowers were recruited. Fritz himself joined in the design work and other craftsmen were attracted by the fascinating game. Josef and Artur Berger designed not only the glass objects, which were then realised by the craftsmen, but also the interior of the Bimini showrooms, display cabinets and even notepaper. Josef designed the little flowerpot logo shown below. Although other artists were associated with Bimini and some of the craftsmen who made the glass items are also known, it was always Fritz Lampl, Josef Berger and Artur Berger who were listed as the artists/designers of Bimini Glass in their catalogues and publicity material (Neuwirth p 462).

 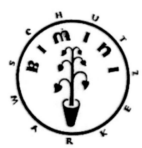 

The name Lampl chose for his company, Bimini, is from a poem by Heinrich Heine (1852) about a fictional island called Bimini, a miracle island where a prince was seeking the spring water of eternal youth. There is also an island in the Caribbean called Bimini.

Bimini Glass

The name and the trademark logo were registered, craftsmen were engaged and the Bimini Workshop was set up. The date was November 1923. In no time magazines were showing illustrations of Bimini glass and stores were selling examples.

Labels displaying the Bimini logo were fixed to each of the creations from the workshop. Unfortunately these tended to fall off, making later identification difficult. There have been many imitators of Bimini both before and after World War II. The name Bimini Glass has come to be used as a generic term for any delicate lamp blown glass from Continental Europe prior to World War II. A simple search of on-line auctions will usually show up a considerable assortment of examples of the Bimini name applied to items not at all likely to have been made by Bimini..

Josef Berger was an advocate of Modernist design principles both in his architecture and his glass designs, which were flowing and simple, without excessive ornamentation. The drawing below is an original design by Josef Berger for the vase "Demeter". He wrote an account of Bimini and Orplid shortly before his death in 1989, and made the point that he and his brother acted as a restraint to some of what he called the more "kitsch and sentimental aspects of the glass designed for Bimini".

Bimini made a very wide range of glass creations as the following chapters of this book will show. Distinguishing features of Bimini, on the whole, were the delicacy of the lamp blown glass and the elegant design. Identifying genuine Bimini pieces is difficult but there are plenty of good sources of information and we hope this book will provide a guide to easier identification in future. There are catalogues of Bimini glass and lists of the glass exhibited by Bimini at international exhibitions in Paris (1925), London (1934) and Rio de Janiero (1930). These are referred to in Waltraud Neuwirth's book on Bimini glass (page 168) with more than half of that book (pages 170 to 460) devoted to pictures and text from those catalogues and lists. Unfortunately all the pictures on those pages are in black and white, and the essential colour features of the designs cannot be seen there. On those 290 pages there are 449 pictures of different Bimini items identified by catalog number, with many of the pictures showing more than one item. It is almost safe to say that if an item is not shown on those pages, it is not Bimini. But Bimini did produce figures with slight variations, and of the 733 known catalogue designs there are some for which no historical pictures are known. In addition there is no clear indication that catalogue designs were followed during the post WW11 period in London. So there is some latitude for confusion.

Neuwirth in her book showed examples of similar items made by competitors and examples of glass artists who may have had an influence on Bimini. There are over 50 pages showing non-Bimini items, interspersed with a few Bimini items for comparison. The text is all in German for those pages, and readers who do not understand German can be forgiven for thinking those items were also by Bimini. If you are using the Neuwirth book as a reference for identifying Bimini (and it is the only book where you will find all those catalogue details) then the pictures are only Bimini if the text underneath says *Bimini-Model Nr.* followed by the model number or alternatively *Bimini-Model Nr. unbekannt, Kat. Nr.* (meaning the model number is unknown but there is a catalog number). The phrase *"Provenienz unbekannt"* under a picture means it has not been identified; it is unlikely to be Bimini. We hope this is helpful. And to avoid adding further to the confusion, all the pictures in this present book are known to be Bimini or Orplid (the later name which was registered in London).

The success of the Bimini Workshop was rapid and considerable, gaining a gold first prize and three silver second prizes for art glass at the Paris Exposition des Arts Decoratifs in 1925, less than 18 months after starting up from scratch. They were competing against the leading glass artists of the day, Lalique, Loetz, Venini, Val St Lambert, Argy-Rousseau, and the Galle Company, amongst many others. This was the exhibition which gave rise to the name Art Deco. Bimini Glass was also exhibited at the Leipzig Fair, the Vienna Fair, and many venues throughout Europe and the USA. In Vienna the Bimini showrooms moved into more prestigious premises as their success grew, eventually being set up in the Stubenring, a very fashionable address near the Museum of Arts and Crafts. Their glass became collectors' items and the Bimini popularity and fame grew. Most of the early customers were affluent Viennese who were delighted by the beauty and optimism shown in Bimini glass. Some no doubt invested in art glass and other art as a hedge against the rampant inflation which had reached a peak in Vienna in August 1922. As Bimini fame spread more orders came from overseas; from Paris, from London, and from the USA. One noteworthy client was George Schenker, known to his friends as "The Playboy of Vienna". He commissioned beautiful drinking glasses from Bimini, and when Fritz needed money to build the showroom and develop the business Schenker offered funds in return for a partnership, which Fritz reluctantly accepted

Although it can be difficult to identify Bimini glass, especially some of the latticino-style goblets, there are many very distinctive features of Bimini items which are not readily found in the work of other glass artists. The chapters in this book display a comprehensive array of Bimini designs. But here we are selecting a few which we hope can help to distinguish Bimini glass.

Bimini made elegant vases, some with very distinctive shaded colouring and some with delicate curling handles or decorative attachments. The examples (below) are from Pipin Henzl's collection in Vienna. The three on the left are Bimini Model no. 3, named "Ceres". The one on the right was named "Phobe" and is Bimini Model number 5. More details of the Bimini glass pictured in this chapter are in a list at the end of the chapter. The kind of coloured glass used in these vases was termed "chrysopras" by Bimini. Black and white pictures of these vases do not show the shading of the colour, an essential feature of the identity and their beauty.

The three vases below show the same Bimini colour shading scheme in different hues and designs. This kind of shading effect together with the designs shown in the Bimini catalogues clearly indicate Bimini creations.

Fantasy items were another trademark of Bimini design. The little "Delphin" vase on the left below and the stunning "Samos" candlestick with a figure of Pegasus in its centre are uniquely Bimini. The decorative glass with a swan in its stem was called "Bacchus" Although the glass is latticino style, with white stripes in clear glass, they are unlike anything made elsewhere even in Venice. These were amongst the glass items shown in the Paris Exposition of 1925. Their success was immediate. .

Other very distinctive designs from Bimini were their delicate and beautiful figurines. Below are "Two Dancers" and "Josephine Baker", who was a famous dancer in Europe in the 1920s. The first woman to dance semi-nude in public at that time, she danced in Vienna in 1928 at a review in the Johann Strauss Theatre. There is a photograph of her with a dedication to Fritz Lampl in her own handwriting which was exhibited in 1980 by the Vienna Theatre Museum (Neuwirth p.466). Fritz went one better than a photograph when he created her image in glass.

Bimini figurines epitomise Fritz Lampl's fascination with capturing the movement and poise of human figures in the "frozen poetry" of glass. Most Bimini figurines use only one colour, and only rarely more than two. There is authenticity in movement and posture; they tend to be abstract and lack detailed features. Bimini figures have a simple egg-shaped head, sometimes with three or more glass curves swept back and upwards to represent hair. And always they convey a feeling, an emotion, and movement.

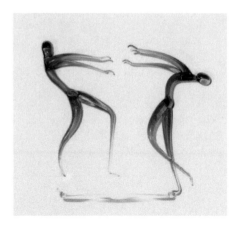

Here are some of Bimini's sensitively poignant animal figures, snake, elephant, gazelles and dog. Notice that the snake has a pattern of circles and also it has teeth. Bimini snakes came in several different pastel colours but never with stripes and always with teeth. Many other glass artists and studios have made glass animals, but the design details and colour schemes used by Bimini are relatively unique and to a trained eye distinctive..

We know that nearly a thousand different Bimini designs were produced, yet there are many more attributed to the Viennese Bimini workshop. Part of the explanation for this is that although Bimini glass proved a huge international success yet it was hard to identify as the labels tended to fall off and very little identifying literature was originally written in English. Mistakes were made years ago, and some items have come to be accepted as Bimini which are definitely questionable. In fact the name has become almost a generic term for all kinds of delicate glassware. Some items which are not Bimini have been so frequently accepted as such that they have become part of a Bimini lore. "Bimini style" may have become a classification, an identity in its own right.

The fame and international reputation of the Bimini workshop grew throughout the late 1920s and early 1930s. In 1929 and 1930 an exhibition of Bimini glass was shown to great acclaim in many major cities across the USA. The number of designers and glass artists involved grew and their showrooms moved ever upwards in status and prestigious location. But Bimini was to be overtaken by world events, and the rise of Nazism in Austria meant that it became unsafe for people of Jewish origin to live and work in Vienna.

Leaving Vienna

In "Red Vienna" the right wing politicians and the very rich were afraid of the power of the Social Democratic Workers Party based on its grass roots support from the well-organised workers. They feared a revolution like the Bolshevik takeover of Russia. They also feared that Hitler's National Socialist Party in Germany would send troops into Austria if given an excuse to suppress the socialists. In 1933-34 Federal Chancellor Engelbert Dollfuss, seeking support from Mussolini in Italy, set about destroying the power of the workers and the Social Democratic Party in Vienna. Through a political manoeuvre in March 1933 he suspended the Austrian Parliament and threatened military force against parliamentarians should they try to reinstate it. He continued to rule by decree and began suspending civil liberties. He banned the Schutzbund, a paramilitary organisation whose purpose included defending the Social Democratic Workers Party, and imprisoned many of its members. In February 1934 another paramilitary organisation, the right-wing Heimwehr encouraged by Dollfuss, attacked a number of buildings looking to seize arms from the Schutzbund. After several skirmishes in different places, members of the Schutzbund in Vienna barricaded themselves in workers' housing estates such as the Karl-Marx-Hof. Dollfuss ordered the Austrian armed forces to shell the Karl-Marx-Hof with machine guns and artillery (Zweig) and this action forced the surrender of the socialist fighters and the end of their power in Vienna for a long time to come.

Staunch supporters of the Socialist Democratic Workers Party, Josef Berger and his wife Margarete were horrified to hear of the army fighting with the workers in Vienna. Josef took up an architectural commission to design an hotel in Haifa and together they left for Palestine in 1934. The situation in Palestine was a big disappointment to them, with open racial hatred between the Arabs and the Jews, and poor administration by the British. In less than a year Margarete left for England while Josef stayed until he had finished his commission in 1936.

Josef's brother Artur Berger had left Vienna in 1936, heading north to Russia, and their sister Fritzi Berger-Hohenberg sailed to the USA about the same time. Old Simon Berger their father had been left a widower and he moved in to live with the Lampls while the Bimini workshop continued for as long as it could.

Flight to London

Fritz Lampl did not leave Vienna until Germany annexed Austria (the Anschluss) in 1938 and the Fascist Austrian Government decreed that non-Aryans could no longer operate a business there. He joined the queue of alarmed Jews who hoped to emigrate to England. The British authorities were encouraging craftsmen to come to Britain; they were not accepting many merchants, office workers nor shop assistants. Fritz wisely took some samples of Bimini glasses and photos of his wife's model dresses to the interview, and with enormous relief gained a visa for himself and his wife.

By this time secret Nazi organisations had penetrated Viennese society and people in Vienna stopped trusting one another. Life-long friends turned their backs on Jewish friends in the street for fear of being seen as associating with Jewish people. Fritz and Hilde made their preparations to leave in secrecy. They went by train on Sunday 3rd July 1938 taking with them Hilde's father and just a few belongings including some precious examples of Bimini glass.

Fritz left the Bimini business to his assistant Maria Gunter. In recent years the Holocaust Centre in Vienna sent Raymond Berger a copy of the letter Fritz Lampl wrote her, calmly handing over the reins for the company.They left so secretly that she had no idea he was going, and arrived for work at the Bimini shop in the Schubertring to find that her boss had fled. Maria tried in vain to "Aryanise" the business but it was nevertheless closed down by Viennese authorities after only a few months. She donated examples of Bimini glass to the Applied Arts Museum in Vienna and the rest were sold to pay her salary and other debts.

The set up in London

When the Lampl's arrived in London they went to stay with Josef and Margarete Berger in Randolph Avenue, Maida Vale. Margarete had been in London since 1935 awaiting Josef on completion of his commission in Palestine. In addition to finding and setting up a home for herself and Josef, she had successfully exhibited her paintings notably at the Austria Shop near New Bond Street, London. A notice in The Times (4th April 1936) reported "Austrian Water-colours: a combination of directness and truth of values makes attractive the 28 water-colours by Mrs. Margarete Hamerschlag ...." Another notice, this one in the Jewish Chronicle, written by Peter Stone (10th April 1936) under the heading – "Margarete Hamerschlag delightful landscapes" gives more praise "The water-colours by the Austro-Jewish artist ....show freshness of vision and the even rarer quality of happiness. One feels a personality in love with life and gifted with the ability to set down that love articulately and with discipline. These little landscapes ….reflect the charm and gaiety of nature without diluting its strength, and the sterner moods are never coarse or brutal…..." An example of Margarete's paintings from that time is this landscape of a port scene probably from Palestine.

Margarete sold three paintings from her first exhibition, earning enough to pay the rent of her house for six weeks. She continued with exhibitions of her work and commissions for portraits but she relied on remissions from Josef for enough money to survive in London. When in 1936 Josef arrived from Palestine and joined her things became more settled. They rented a studio in Gt. Chapel Street, Soho, where Josef made and displayed his designs in modernist furniture and sought commissions as an architect. In 1937 their son Raymond was born. By the time the Lampl's arrived in July 1938 they were able to welcome them to stay in their home while Fritz found a house for Hilde and himself, and a floor of the building where Josef had his workshop became the Bimini workshop in London. Hilde Berger-Lampl set up her dress design and dress making workshop in the same building.

Within a matter of days the news that Fritz Lampl, the famous artist-designer, had moved to London was announced in the News Chronicle (Monday July 11th) and his fame as the "Poet in Glass" was reported. The new Bimini Glass workshop in Gt. Chapel Street was soon set up, and by November 1938 Fritz Lampl was registered as a "qualified designer for industry" in the National Register of Industrial Art Designers.

Fritz soon had many friends in London and when he rented a house in Hampstead (an affluent suburb just north of the city) his home became a popular meeting place for other émigrés from Vienna. His good friend Lucie Rie arrived in London in October with her husband Hans. In Vienna Fritz had displayed Lucie Rie's pottery in the Bimini shop on the Schubertring and she had won prizes for her pottery at some of the same international Exhibitions and Trade Fairs as Bimini. They were animated, enthusiastic friends and supported and encouraged one another throughout the Lampl's time in London. Lucie was at his bedside many years later when he died in hospital.

Bimini Glass

Exotic and luxury items were heavily taxed in Britain and not the kind of product range that would find favour with the UK Board of Trade, a government department with enormous power to control the output of manufacturers in preparation for war. Some of the Bimini range of glass items were not made or only rarely made in London. Glass animals, for example, which had been a very popular line for the Viennese Bimini workshop, could only be made in London if they were for "Export Only" (Pathe News 1945.). In an interview Fritz Lampl explained that when he was asked to provide glass animals for a performance of "The Glass Menagerie" in London he had to tell them he no longer made glass animals and indeed he had none in his possession.

Fritz recognized that whilst war time restrictions ruled out some of his designs they also opened up new opportunities. Fritz was eager to help other émigrés from his home country by providing them with work at his glass studio. His glass was still delicate and beautiful but aimed to be practical in its applications. Glassware for domestic use was allowed; beautiful sculptures and vases were not. Few if any of the refugees fleeing from the Nazis were skilled in glass blowing. If he was to offer them work it had to be fairly unskilled. Making glass buttons was just such an opportunity. They were easy to make and since hostilities in Europe meant that imports from Czechoslovakia had ceased there was a huge shortage of glass buttons and costume jewelry in glass formerly imported from that country. No doubt Hilde's dress designs helped to draw the Lampl's attention to the need for well-designed buttons. Fashion houses and film studios in London wanted high quality buttons to decorate their costumes. Soon Fritz's Bimini buttons, brooches and glass jewelry were in demand around the free world. He was able to offer work to Austrian refugees to help them get started in London. Lucie Rie was one of those people, but after a very short effort to make glass buttons she turned to her own specialism of pottery, and proceeded to make ceramic buttons and ceramic components for Bimini glass buttons.

William Honey, a curator at the Victoria and Albert Museum in London, was a friend to both Lucie Rie and Fritz Lampl, and encouraged them by allowing medals and coins in the museum collection to be pressed into plaster molds so making templates for button designs. Hot glass was pressed into these plaster molds to reproduce the designs from ancient treasures as glass and ceramic buttons and brooches. They proved very popular. A brass button back was designed with the little Bimini flower pot logo together with "MADE IN ENGLAND". During the years Bimini was incorporated as a UK limited company (1941 to 1948) "BIMINI Ltd" was added and the flower pot logo had a circle around it with the words Bimini Limited. Here are some examples. The one in the centre is a Lucie Rie ceramic brooch with the Bimini flowerpot logo.

Bimini Glass

Here are some of the Bimini buttons based on museum items such as ancient coins and medallions..

Fritz also employed skilled British glass blowers at the Bimini workshop in London. They made a range of beautiful goblets and flasks and other practical items. Latticino style items with white stripes on clear glass were popular. The mustard pot with cover and a hole for a spoon is an excellent example of the kind of practical item which gained Board of Trade approval even in wartime (author Raymond's collection).

One of the first skilled glass blowers employed by Bimini Ltd. at the Soho workshop was Ellen Turner, who had worked in the glass industry for many years but was out of work at the time. Her grand-daughter Pauline told me in an interview in 2006 that her "Nan" surprised the family one day in 1939 when she said she was going up to London "to get a job". She returned later that day to confirm she was now employed at the Bimini Glass workshop in Soho. Ellen also obtained a job for her daughter Peggy working in the office at Bimini. One of Peggy's tasks was to hand deliver expensive buttons that had been made especially for customers who could afford to pay a high price for hand-made exclusives She particularly remembered taking a large coat button to film star Margaret Lockwood at her hotel in London. The price for that one button was thirty pounds, an outrageous sum of money to spend in those days.

The "Playboy of Vienna" Georg Karpeles-Schenker turned up in Soho with money to invest in return for a partnership, and Fritz reluctantly accepted (Josef Berger manuscript). Always referred to as "Mr. Schenker" by those who worked for him, his business skills were useful to Fritz, as was his willingness to "manage" the workshop while Fritz was busy entertaining friends or concentrating on his glass designing. Mr. Schenker encouraged Lucie Rie when she set up a little pottery workshop beneath her flat in Albion Mews and in particular encouraged her to make ceramic components for the Bimini buttons and jewelry (Birks p 38). Lucie was grateful to Fritz for giving her work at the button factory, and divided her time between her own little studio and her "day job" at the button workshop.

The situation in Europe was worsening all this time, and on 3 September 1939 when Germany ignored an ultimatum to cease military operations against Poland, the United Kingdom, France, Australia and New Zealand declared war on Germany. They were joined shortly afterwards by South Africa and Canada. This was a war in which civilians going about their daily lives were bombed from the air by enemy aircraft. Our artist family and their friends were caught in the middle of it. War was no longer an affair fought between military protagonists. Men, women and children were under direct attack. Windows were blacked out and lights extinguished so the enemy planes could not see their targets. Gas masks were distributed to everyone. Air raid shelters were set up deep in London's underground stations. And civilians were trained in firefighting, rescue and first aid. Even Lucie Rie, who spoke very little English, became a firefighter.

As the battles in Europe raged through countries just across the English Channel fear grew in Britain of invasion by Germany. There were suspicions of German spies entering the country as refugees and preparing to assist Germany in their invasion. This fear that there was a "fifth column" of enemy aliens grew to fever pitch in Britain. An attempt was made to classify "aliens" according to their degree of risk, with high risk potential threats given "A" category status, B category being moderate risk, and those presenting no risk at all C category. There followed an elaborate and time consuming process of interviews and classification which was abandoned in early 1940 as taking too long. A decree was passed that all Germans and Austrians between 16 and 60 were to be interned, a process which started in May 1940. The Isle of Man was chosen as the location for this internment and some ships of internees were sent to the British colonies of Canada and Australia.

When Italy entered the war on June 11th 1940 all the Italians in Britain were instantly classified as enemy aliens to be interned, such were their fears. A week later it was reported to Parliament that only 12000 of 76000 Germans and Austrians and less than a third of 15,000 Italians had been interned. This was not acceptable progress and Churchill's Cabinet ordered the immediate internment of all male enemy aliens between 16 and 60. This wholesale rounding up started in June 1940. Schoolboys and the sick were to be exempt, but there was such chaos when the police and armed forces set about implementing this policy that many schoolboys, old men over 60 and invalids were arrested and sent to internment camps.

On the 21st of June 1940 Josef Berger and Fritz Lampl were declared enemy aliens and sent to be detained at Camp Mooragh, the first of several Isle of Man internment camps. The "camps" were comprised of sea-front boarding houses connected together and surrounded by barbed-wire fences. Other nearby houses would be commandeered for the guards who were put in charge. Observers described the long line of men disembarking onto the pier carrying their belongings. Some were smart professional types wearing suits, others wore their working clothes, and some were young schoolboys still in short trousers. One man carried a typewriter, another a fishing rod and one had even brought his dog (Chappell). Some of the internees were clearly unfit. Mooragh Camp was only for Germans and Austrians; they had to share bedrooms and Josef and Fritz were room-mates.

This whole process of arresting and interning all Germans and Austrians indiscriminately seemed cruel and unjust. Men who had escaped persecution by the Nazis in Europe were thrown together with German prisoners of war and fascists who hated them and continued to abuse them when they could. It was reported to have been worse on board the internment ships heading for the colonies. In the boarding houses of the Isle of Man the guards tried to keep violence and aggression under control. Eventually the Nazis and Fascists were separated into one camp away from the others on the island (Chappell).

From the start of the internment camps those who had professional experience or expertise shared their knowledge with other inmates. Hundreds carried their chairs to lectures in the evenings (Chappell). Josef Berger, by that time a respected member of the Royal Institute of British Architecture (RIBA) gave lectures on building construction and architectural planning. Fritz was released after only a few months because of his life-long ill health. He was sent home on September 9th 1940. Josef had to wait longer, and his case was taken up by senior spokesmen for the RIBA, Professor Sir Charles Reilly and Lord Lytton (Pholz). They argued that his architectural skills were valuable to the country and his opposition to Fascism in Vienna was a matter of record. Before he was released in January 1941, however, his studio in Gt. Chapel Street had been destroyed by an enemy bomb.

It was Fritz, accompanied by Lucie Rie, who found the studio destroyed. Arriving there for work, Fritz from his house in Hampstead and Lucie from her flat in Albion Mews, they were appalled to discover that a bomb had scored a direct hit on the building during the night and there was only one partial wall left standing. Lucie recorded poignantly some years later that the only item left undamaged was her potter's apron which was hanging from a hook on the remnants of that wall (Birks, page 38).

Fritz set up a small glassblowing operation in the basement of his house in Hampstead as a temporary arrangement to keep Bimini going. With financial help from his partner George Schenker he set about re-creating the Bimini glass studio. The new venue was not very far from Albion Mews where Lucie Rie had her studio and she was delighted he had moved nearer to her studio (Birks).

Josef Berger had also lost his studio when the Gt. Chapel Street building was bombed. He was helped by his friends in the RIBA and found work with Professor Abercrombie on the staff of London County Council where his theories of architectural planning were put to good use. He worked on a major endeavor for rebuilding London after the war and a substantial book and film were produced on the subject. His specialism became the design of new schools in the London area.

The name Bimini was established as a UK limited company, incorporated on the 9th May 1941 and registered at the new address 10 Mount Row, Mayfair. The Austrian registration of the name Bimini should have been valid until 1943, but the Bimini Company in Austria was terminated by the Austrian authorities in 1940.
Ellen Turner and her daughter Peggy moved with Bimini to the new workshop which they proudly described as a two storey building "just off Park Lane". It was the kind of prestigious business address in an attractively designed building that would appeal very much to Fritz and Mr. Schenker. Pauline used to visit her "Mum" at Mount Row and wait for her in the office. There were 8 people working there, whom she described as "elderly types" which probably meant they were middle aged, as Pauline was only young then. George Schenker was managing the factory and in her opinion "he fancied Mum" who was always dressed very smartly and was not married at the time. She described Mr. Schenker as a "fly boy" (which matches his reputation as the "Playboy of Vienna") who always carried a roll of money in one pocket and a packet of treats in his other pocket.

Meantime Lucie Rie, encouraged by George Schenker, was producing some beautiful ceramic buttons and jewelry at her little studio and by 1940 was doing so well that she took on two assistants. However in 1941 the UK Board of Trade decided hers was a non-essential industry and closed down her workshop. Lucie was sent to work for the war effort in an optical instruments factory. However before and after her shifts for this company Lucie made buttons and parts for buttons and jewelry for Bimini. She was not allowed to re-open her own studio until after the war, in late 1945.

This was just a small part of the massive war effort in Britain. All industries were required to contribute, and factories were converted to making munitions, components for military and defence equipment, products for the armed forces, and essential domestic goods. Glass factories were partially closed and converted to making products like glass screens for radar, glass prisms for spotlights, laboratory glassware, optical instruments, even down to making beer glasses for the armed forces.

Here are some of the beautiful ceramic and glass buttons and brooches which Bimini Glass produced with Lucie's input.

And of course, the Bimini output wasn't all buttons. Fritz and Ellen Turner, working at the new premises, were making beautiful glasses, flasks, bottles and decanters, all with a practical application It was not until after the war that they were able to produce some of their more glamorous items.. Here is one of the perfume bottles with a cupid figure inside that were made during those years in London.

This example is from Raymond Berger's collection. He has a photograph of another similar bottle but sadly only the photograph now exists. On the back in Fritz Lampl's handwriting it says: *Perfume Bottle "Cupid". The glass figure of Cupid is cast inside. Bottle clear crystal. Figure white opaque. Spots on stopper gold, so is the heart on the outside. Priced at 30/- (£1.50) Glass. Handmade in England.*

Ellen Turner's daughter Peggy was working in the Bimini office during the war, and whenever her fiancé, Charles Hume, came home on leave he also used to visit Peggy at the glassworks. He was a technical specialist employed by the Navy fitting radar to ships. This was very new technology and "Chas" was much in demand for his expertise. He told me that when he visited Bimini "I was introduced to a Mr. Schenker, and he _was_ Bimini Glass, but there was another man there, Mr. Lampl". It was Mr. Schenker who managed the workforce and was in daily contact with the workers. Chas described the workers as "Matronly women who looked as though they had never worked in their lives". Chas became friendly with Fritz and used to give advice on technical problems with the burners or the products. When Charles and Peggy decided to get married Mr. Schenker went with them to Covent Garden to advise on the jewels and delighted them by paying for their engagement ring (which cost 75 pounds).

After the war in 1946 Mr. Schenker and Fritz invited Chas to work at the factory. Schenker wanted Chas to take over managing the production process and the workforce, and even though he believed the offer was only an act of charity he took the job when he was "de-mobbed". He was not optimistic about his chances for improving the productivity of the factory. He told me many years later "I can still see those workers in my mind's eye, typical refugees who had been used to money. I thought I'd never be able to get a day's work out of them". But he took on the job and tried to improve things. Unfortunately this was at a time when other British glassworks were making inroads into the Bimini monopoly for handmade glass buttons and jewelry. Glass Developments Ltd in Brixton for example produced a range of glass buttons with brass backs very similar to the Bimini ones. The additional cost of taking on a manager cut further into the Bimini profits. Chas struggled for six months to organize and increase production at Bimini but eventually decided that there was no future for him at the factory.

The Bimini company, meantime, continued to attract attention for high quality glass and imaginative designs. In 1946 they were invited to exhibit at the "Britain Can Make it" Exhibition, organized by the UK Design Council with the aim of attracting overseas buyers to Buy British. The following year in 1947 Bimini was listed as an exhibitor in the British Industries Fair in London. The company was described as "Manufacturers of hand-made glass and pottery buttons which are unique in design and quality. Each piece is an individual work of Hand-Craftsmanship in Glass or Pottery." (Grace's Guide).

In 1947 when Charles Hume resigned and took with him his wife Peggy and Ellen Turner they formed a company of their own and set up a workshop in an old cinema building in Walthamstow. From 1949 onwards they were listed in trade directories as **Chatur and Company Ltd.** (Cha from Charles and tur from Turner) **making "Pressed Glass". T**hey worked with clear borosilicate glass and acetylene torches, a different process from Bimini, but their range of glass buttons, scarf rings and hat pins was essentially in competition with Bimini. They also made glass animals. Even when the huge Czechoslovakian glass factories re-started selling glass buttons into Britain in the 1950s, Chatur Ltd. survived for many years by being creative and switching to other products.

Meanwhile when Ellen Turner, Peggy and Charles Hume resigned from Bimini George Schenker was left managing the partially skilled refugee workforce whose productivity was poor. The company was now facing increased competition in Britain and the threat of an influx of glass buttons from Europe once trade restrictions were lifted. They were lifted early in the 1950s. Schenker who had visited the USA in 1945 aboard the Cunard ship EDAM had talked with American button manufacturers and made contact with a company who supplied automated button making machines. In 1947 he thought it was a good idea to purchase automated button-making machinery for Bimini with the company's money. This was not the time for such an investment, and the very idea of a factory for automated button making ran completely counter to Fritz Lampl's self-image. He was very angry about the money, and totally opposed to converting Bimini into an automated factory. This was the final straw and the partnership was ended. The Bimini operation in Manor Way closed down and Fritz moved the glass workshop to Hampstead. The name Bimini was abandoned and a new name was registered in 1948 – Orplid Glass Ltd. with Fritz as the managing director and his wife Hilde the secretary. **Bimini Limited was "liquidated" from the register of UK limited companies on April 11th 1949.**

WOMEN'S WEAR NEWS, August 25, 1949   27

HAND-MADE BUTTONS OF SINGULAR BEAUTY

Designs in Blown Glass

THE rich fabrics and glowing colours of the new Autumn fashions have created a need for buttons that break away from their strictly utilitarian purpose and are both unusual and exciting.

This need is being filled by the efforts of the **Orplid Glass Co.**, Ferncroft-avenue, Hampstead. Here are produced handmade buttons with the singular beauty that is imbued by the skilled craftsman.

Most of them are made from blown glass which has a delicate bubble-like appearance but is, in actual fact, quite strong.

The shapes, sizes and designs are numerous. There are global, round, square, oblong and oval buttons. Some resemble stars, others shells, scrolls, hearts, leaves or half-moons. Enchanting are those in the form of animals, fish or birds. All are gilded with little spikes or tracery.

Jewel colourings, ruby, sapphire or emerald add to their exotic appearance.

Another type of button is imprinted with steel dyed motifs from coins dating back to 400 B.C.

Attractive jewellery is also featured. Necklaces of graduated global buttons on black velvet ribbon, matched with ear-clips and spiky hat pins. Cameo fobs, tiny perfume bottles to be carried in the handbag or with a pin attachment for wear on the lapel.

Top: a selection of novelty buttons and jewellery fashioned by the Orplid Glass Co.

The buttons take the form of a fish, dice, the wings of a sycamore seed, spiked cube, shell, clover leaf and a heart. They are made in coloured and gilded handblown glass.

Both the hat pin and the perfume bottle, which has a pin attachment for wear on the lapel, are made in blown glass and decorated with tiny gold spikes.

Left: buttons and jewellery made by Lucie Rie, who works in co-operation with the Orplid Glass Co.

The buttons are made in glazed and gilded pottery in a number of effective and unusual designs. Also in gilded pottery are the shell-like hat pin, buckle, and ear-ring and collar set. The latter fastens at the back of the neck with black velvet ribbon.

Working in co-operation with the Orplid Glass Co., is Lucie Rie of Albion Mews, Albion-street. Buttons fashioned from glazed and gilded pottery are the speciality here.

These too, cover the whole range of shapes, sizes and designs and as befits the material are chunky. Practically a complete zoo of animals has been created.

Colours are made by the artist herself to customer's requirements. Gold, brown and beige are the most popular shades at present. Delightful smoky blues, moss greens and raspberry pinks are also available. Buckles for both shoes and belts, hat pins, ear-clips, brooches, tassel knobs and gilt collars on velvet ribbons are other items made in pottery.

These artists are proof that craftsmanship still exists. Not only that, but they are helping to give English clothes an elegance and distinction that will earn them applause in the realms of the fashion world.

Under the new name "Orplid" Fritz re built his glass workshop in the basement of their home in Hampstead, and even installed a kiln so Lucie Rie could continue making her ceramics for the Orplid range of buttons and jewellery. The social life at the Lampl house continued and refugees from Europe were given jobs in this workshop to help them get started in their new country. The name, Orplid Glass, was derived from a poem written by E. Morike about a magical country called Orplid. This new name soon appeared in fashion and design magazines. The article above is from Women's Wear News in August 1949. They wrote "This need is being filled by the efforts of the Orplid Glass Company, Ferncroft avenue, Hampstead. Here are produced handmade buttons with the singular beauty that is imbued by the skilled crafts-man. ...... Working in co-operation with the Orplid Glass Co. is Lucie Rie of Albion Mews."

Raymond Berger remembers a time when an unexploded bomb was found near their Paddington home and he and his parents went to stay with the Lampl's in Hampstead for a few days. They had to vacate their house for a time. Raymond remembers that glass working was taking place in the basement where he saw Bunsen burners being used..

As a child Raymond was well acquainted with Fritz Lampl and liked him immensely. He enjoyed Fritz's sense of humour and Fritz, who had no children of his own, liked having Raymond around. He wrote: "My parents and I were often at the Lampls rather grand home in Hampstead but as a small child with virtually no knowledge of German I amused myself as best I could while the adults chatted on over coffee and cigarettes. The house had a pall of cigarette smoke about it."

Orplid Glass was successful in the UK and overseas. Glass jewelry, buttons and brooches, drinking glasses, jugs and decanters were enthusiastically displayed in upmarket stores such as Heals and Harrods, and were getting very favourable reviews in the design magazines. His glass was frequently featured in the press. Orplid Glass was one of the products selected to represent the revival of Post-war design in Britain at the Festival of Britain in 1951, and Fritz had a display stand by invitation at this huge exhibition. The wine glass shown below with a swan stem, is a fine example of Orplid Glass created in London during those heady days.

Fritz built up his workshop again, still giving help to European refugees and employing British glass artisans like Ben George, who was featured in an article in the magazine John Bull in 1950. Ben George had been a glass blower making laboratory glass for Clarendon Laboratory in Oxford. He saw a magazine article about Fritz Lampl's blown glass creations and contacted Fritz, who employed him in a new Orplid workshop he was setting up in Oxford. Orplid Glass grew, and in the 1950s Fritz also had a workshop in Kilburn.

Orplid Glass in the 1950s

As the fifties saw the re-emergence of mass produced glass imports from Central Europe which had been halted by the War the market became inundated with cheap glassware. Orplid's monopoly was soon broken. Lampl's small hand-made operations could not compete with mass-produced imports from countries such as Czechoslovakia and the company began to struggle. Fritz and Hilde's financial problems were made worse when the secretary Hilde had employed to help with bookwork stole most of their savings. Although the thief was caught and sent to prison the money was never recovered. Fritz closed down his workshop in Kilburn, sold the stock and also closed the workshop in Oxford.

Both Bimini and Orplid had always been small scale studio-based operations. Trying to compete with mass produced glass from Europe was too much for Fritz Lampl. The new imports were cheaper, very colourful and available in large quantities. The effort sapped his capital and his health - never robust, finally gave out. He died of a heart attack in 1955, and his wife Hilde followed him a few weeks later. The Bimini/Orplid studio finally closed and only the legacy of their beautiful glass continues.

When they died in 1955 Josef Berger (Raymond's father) was Fritz and Hilde's closest relative. He invited their many friends to take away something from the house to remember them by, and eventually the Bergers were left with the remainder of the stock which had not been sold nor given away. This consisted mostly of sample drawers full of buttons and small glass items intended to be made into jewelry and a small number of glassware items. The house itself was only rented and there were outstanding debts for Josef to pay.

Epitaph

The remaining four from our peer group of Viennese artists all continued with successful careers. Artur Berger kept a low profile in Stalin's Russia to avoid persecution in the early years, but went on to become a famous film art director in that country. Fritzi Berger-Hohenberg was a successful dress designer in the US and took back to the States Hilde's remaining dress samples after the funeral. Josef Berger's work for the London County Council implemented his theories of architectural planning for new schools in London; He is particularly known for his designs for Woodbury Down School, where he pioneered the process of interviewing teachers who were to work in the new school so that their views on what was needed were incorporated into the design. And just as successful in a different way was Margarete Berger-Hamerschlag who used her art to influence young people in poor neighbourhoods in London. She was involved in the early days of "Youth Clubs" in the UK just after the war, an idea that grew into an institution for involving teenagers in positive activities to "get them off the streets". Margarete's illustrated book about her work teaching art in Youth Clubs became a best seller and was reprinted several times in the UK and overseas (Berger-Hamerschlag *Journey Into a fog*). Lucie Rie was not one of the family, but her close friendship and continued work for Bimini and Orplid meant she was "one of the team". When Fritz Lampl died in hospital she was at his bedside holding his hand. She continued making pottery into her 90s and has been called "the most important potter of the 20th Century:" (Birks) In 1991 she was made a Dame of the British Empire, she turned down an honorary doctorate from the Art College in Vienna but accepted one from Heriot Watt University, Edinburgh in 1992. And when she died, nearly 40 years after Fritz, his photograph was the only one on her wall.

The Bimini legacy lives on, in our memories of the special people who made it and the beautiful glass which will always be a joy. The remainder of this book is devoted to examples of the frozen poetry in glass of Fritz Lampl and his team of artists.

Bimini Glass

LIST OF GLASS ILLUSTRATIONS IN CHAPTER 1

1: Raymond and Sasha Berger by a plaque on workers flats in Vienna designed by their fathers.

2: Margarete Hamerschlag with her sister Nelly in Vienna c. 1914.

3: Josef and Margarete Berger on holiday in Austria

4: Fritzi Berger designs from postcards in the W W series

5: Original design by Josef Berger for the Bimini vase "Demeter".

6: "Ceres" 3 vases, Bimini model 3, Neuwirth catalogue 5-7, height 9.4cm. 10.9cm. and 11.1cm.

7: "Phoebe" vase, Bimini model 5, Neuwirth catalogue 14, height 10.8cm.

8: "Ikaros" vase Bimini model 27, Neuwirth catalogue 93, height 20.3 cm

9: "Danae" vase Bimini model 7, Neuwirth catalogue 18, height 22cm.

10: "Delphin" vase Bimini model 136, Neuwirth catalogue 213, height 17.8cm

11: "Samos" candlestick, Pegasus in centre, Bimini model 149, Neuwirth catalogue 227, height 28cm

12: "Bacchus" vase Bimini model 105, Neuwirth catalogue 175, height 24cm

13: 2 blue dancers, Bimini model 990 f, Neuwirth catalogue +20, height 8cm

14: "Josephine Baker" dancer no Bimini model , Neuwirth catalogue 701, height 8cm

15: Snake: Bimini model , Neuwirth catalogue , height cm

16: Elephant Bimini model 853, Neuwirth catalogue 526, height approx..5cm

17: 2 antelopes Bimini model 721, Neuwirth catalogue 450, height 10cm

18: Dachshund begging -Bimini model 943, Neuwirth catalogue 573, height cm

19: Painting of dock scene by Margarete Hamerschlag in the 1930s.

20: Bimini and Orplid button backs

21: Bimini buttons and scarf ring

22: Orplid honey pot

23: Fritz and Hilde Lampl

24: Bimini buttons with Lucie Rie ceramics.

25: Perfume bottle with cupid inside.

26: Women's Wear News article about Orplid jewelry and buttons

27: Orplid goblet with Swan stem.

2: VASES, GLASSES AND DECANTERS

There exists a huge variety of shapes, colours, sizes and types of glass to be found in Bimini vases and glasses. Sometimes it is hard to believe they were all produced "at the lamp", but we know that all Bimini glass was blown or shaped sitting at a bench using a specialist burner lamp similar to a bunsen burner. Pipin Henzl and his wife Inge started collecting art deco era glass in Vienna during the 1970s. Ten years later Pipin studied the documents and glass collection in the Vienna museum of fine arts (the MAK as it is known) and learned that part of his collection was Bimini glass. From then on he specialized in collecting Bimini and built up the best collection of Bimini currently known. The photograph below shows a small part of his collection on the corner of a specially built display cabinet.

Many of the vases made by Bimini are tall and thin as you can see here. The tallest of these is 39cm and they are all extremely light and delicate. Note the two latticino-style goblets to the right of this picture, with hollow globes in their stems. Named "Ariadne" (Bimini model 119) both goblets have a Bimini label still attached to the base, and the globes are empty. We have never come across an authenticated Bimini goblet with any kind of item inside a globe in the stem – no birds, animals, nor flowers. Bimini made small perfume bottles containing beautiful cupids as shown in chapter 5, but to our knowledge, no creatures in globes in the stems of their goblets.

Bimini examples from Pipin Henzl's collection formed a large part of the Bimini exhibition in Austria in April

1992. Raymond Berger, nephew of Fritz Lampl, was invited to that exhibition as a guest and was amazed at the number of Bimini items that were shown. The exhibition was organized by Dr.Waltraud Neuwirth, former curator at the MAK museum, who launched her book about Bimini Glass at the exhibition. The poster shown here advertised the exhibition. Where we have identified an item in this book with "Neuwirth catalogue" and a number, that refers to the catalogue numbers in Neuwirth's book for this 1992 Exhibition of Bimini glass.

Many Bimini vases are simple classical shapes with beautiful colouring like the examples in Chapter one and these below. The delicate "handles" on the first two are also typical of Bimini design – delicate and beautiful but possibly not very practical. Sizes and details are given in the list of illustrations at the end of this chapter.

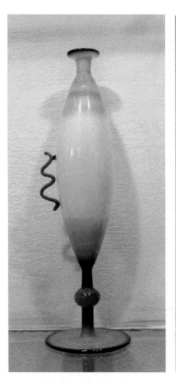

Bimini Glass

This beautiful decanter type vase with heavy trailing in clear glass has both the rare Bimini label and the Fritz Lampl label, which is even more rare. Beside it is a vase with the same kind of thick regular trailing. This second example was made during the company's London period where the name Bimini was used until 1948 when Orplid became the company name. This Orplid vase belongs to Sebastian Gomperts, whose mother Barbara was a friend of Fritz Lampl. Barbara and Fritz shared the same birthday and some of her collection were birthday gifts.

The decanter vase is named "Catull" and is Bimini model 207. The closest example in the Bimini catalogue to this Orplid vase is "Plautus" Bimini model number 206, Neuwirth catalogue number 238.

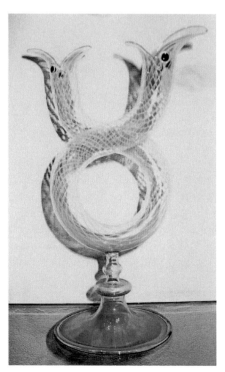

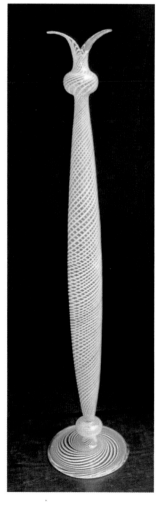

Latticino style glass, clear with white stripes sometimes called filigree glass, was used extensively by Bimini and later by Orplid. Filigrana style, where the stripes are coloured, was also popular. This tall slender latticino style vase measures 36.3cm tall and was named "Orchis". Its Bimini model number is 127.

The fantasy vase on the left is also latticino style with two snake-like heads for openings. It was named "Eleusis" and its Bimini model number is 115. Both of these latticino style vases were exhibited at the Paris Exposition Internationale des Arts Decoratifs in 1925 and in the Exhibition of Austrian Art in London in 1934.

In this next long stemmed vase the white stripes are quite widely spaced. It was named "Rialto" and has a Bimini label attached. The Bimini model number is 145.

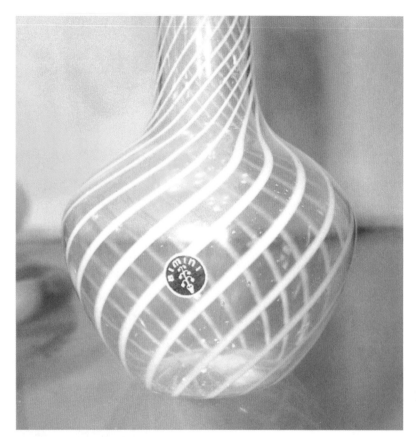
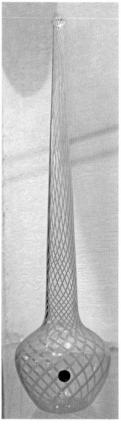

This goblet is more typical of the Bimini latticino style with very fine white lines circling round the glass. It was made in the London period and its hand written label says "Orplid Glass".

Bimini Glass

Another item in latticino style from the Orplid period is this flask with its rare Fritz Lampl label on the base. It measures approximately 24cm tall and 10cm across the base and is part of the small collection inherited by Raymond Berger from his father Josef.

Here are two examples of the Filigrana style by Bimini, where the encircling lines are black on clear glass. This style of glass was very popular during the London era for Bimini/Orplid. The jam or honey pot has a hole in the lid to fit a spoon. This example is from the Gomperts collection. There is an example in chapter one of a white striped Orplid honey pot.

These two latticino glasses, in white stripes on clear glass, were made in the London studio, probably during the Orplid years. They are part of Raymond Berger's collection, as are the four beautiful wine glasses with white twists in their stems and the set of five goblets with black on clear filigrano stems below.

Here are three delightful flowers which do not look like glass, but apart from the two ceramic pots, they are entirely made of glass. The blue tulip vase is all glass. It is part of the Henzl collection and the other two are from the Bimini archives at the MAK museum.

LIST OF ILLUSTRATIONS FOR CHAPTER 2

1: Part of Pipin and Inge Henzl's collection of Bimini glass. All examples in this chapter are from the Henzl collection except Orplid ones, which are from Raymond Berger's collection and others as indicated.

2: Leaflet advertising Bimini exhibition held in Vienna in 1992

3: Neuwirth Catalogue item 21, height 20cm

4: "Diana" vase. Bimini model 4, height 19cm.

5: "Ikaros" vase. Bimini model 57 height 20.3cm

6: "Catull" vase. Bimini model 207 and height 20.3cm

7: Orplid vase similar to "Plautus" Bimini model 206, Neuwirth catalogue item 238, height 16cm.

8: "Eleusis" fantasy vase, Bimini model 115, height 20cm

9: "Orchis" vase, Bimini model 127, **36.3cm tall**

10: "Rialto" vase, Bimini model 145, close up showing Bimini label.

11: "Rialto" vase, Bimini model 145 with label, height 33cm

12: Latticino glass goblet from Orplid period with hand written label on base

13: Base of goblet showing "Orplid Glass" and hard-to-read model name "tratorea"

14: Orplid latticino glass flask which has Fritz Lampl label on base

15: Base of Orplid flask with Fritz Lampl label

16: Honey pot with filigrana black lines on clear glass, Orplid period, Gomperts collection.

17: Goblet with filigrana black lines on clear glass, Orplid period, Gomperts collection.

18: Two Orplid latticino glasses, white stripes on clear glass

19: Four Orplid wine glasses with white twist stems.

20: Five Orplid goblets with black on clear filigrano stems.

21: Blue tulip vase Bimini model 355 height 23.4cm.

22: Yellow tulip vase height 16.25cm Neuwirth catalogue number 286, MAK collection

23: Cactus vase height 13.8cm Neuwirth catalogue number 292, MAK collection.

3: FIGURINES

Bimini figurines are basically stick figures which nevertheless manage to show intense activity and feelings. There are normally no facial features, the heads are simple egg shapes sometimes with stylized hair. We have not come across any authenticated Bimini examples with breasts.

The movement of these dancers is captured with such accuracy that observers can visualise the next moves in the dance. When two or three girls are dancing together as in the pictures below, you can even feel the beat of the music as well as visualize the next steps.

The three blue dancers are Bimini model 996 and the two red dancers are Bimini 998 . Several variants of these models were made, with the arms in different positions. There is a variant of the three blue dancers with their horizontal arms above their heads, and one with their arms at waist height, again horizontal. Most Bimini dancing figurines are approximately 8cm tall.

Bimini figurines include sports activities, figures with animals, and figures going about their day to day activities, as well as the dancers. Here are two examples standing together of the Bimini model named "START" and on the right below is "Fencer claiming victory" (Fechtende, Bimini model 990 y).

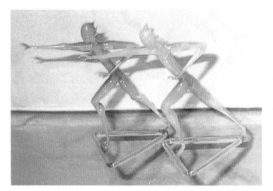 

Here is the Bimini model named JAGD – The Hunt. A similar model without the deer is named "DIANA with Hound".

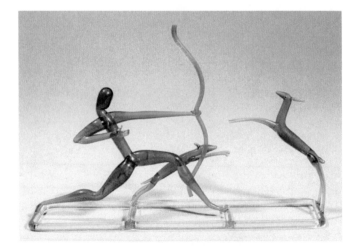

Some of the most beautiful Bimini figurines are those with animals or birds. This girl with a flute playing to a bird is very poignant. It is shown in the Bimini catalogue without a model number.

This figurine of a girl with an antelope is shown in the Neuwirth catalogue as authenticated Bimini, but its model number is not known.

Bimini Glass

Amongst the many day to day activity figurines made by Bimini we have chosen the "Sweep" with his ladder and top hat.

One of the most sensuous and beautiful Bimini figurines is Liebespaar -The Lovers. This photograph of The Lovers sitting on a bench was taken in front of a Bimini vase in the Henzl collection.

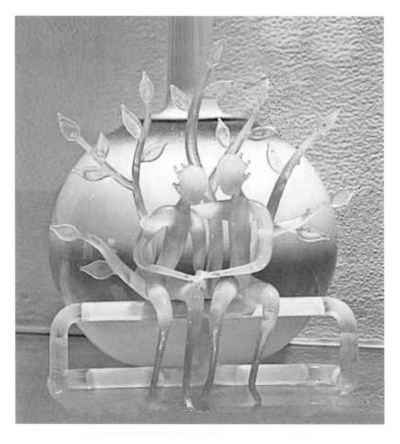

LIST OF ILLUSTRATIONS FOR CHAPTER 3

1: Dancer Bimini model 991 d   Neuwirth catalogue number 650.   Height 8cm.

2: Dancer Neuwirth catalogue 716   Height 9.7cm

3: Three blue dancers Bimini model 996 (variant), Neuwirth catalogue 684, height 8cm.

4: Two red dancers Bimini model 998,   Neuwirth catalogue 719, height 8cm.

5: START 2 examples of Bimini model named "START   Neuwirth catalogue 714 and 715, height 7cm.

6: Fencers (Fechtende) Bimini model 990 y. Neuwirth catalogue 646, height 8cm.

7: Hunt. Bimini model 996 f , Neuwirth catalogue 691, height 7.4cm and length 11.4cm.

8: Girl with flute, Neuwirth catalogue item 724, height 4.5cm.

9: Girl with antelope, Neuwirth catalogue 730, height 7.9cm.

10: Sweep. Neuwirth catalogue 721, height 8.3cm

11. Liebespaar (the lovers) Bimini model 999 variant, Neuwirth catalogue number 711, height 8.9cm .

4: EXOTIC ANIMALS, BIRDS AND OTHERS

Bimini glass animals and birds are exotic as well as beautiful, and exude personality. Here are three that show the variety of styles: the black horse with his expressive posture and face; the elephant in typical Bimini colours of soft brown patches on a cream base; and the mythical animal that looks like a unicorn.

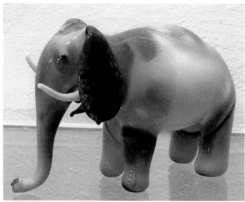

The horse is about four and a half centimeters high, the elephant six and a half and the unicorn 20cm. At the other extreme for size are the grasshopper and the hedgehog, each only two and a half centimeters tall.

Birds were popular Bimini figurines. Here are the magpie, an owl and a pair of pelicans. The look of sheer dejection expressed by the magpie conveys such a sense of emotion you can almost hear him sigh.

This little spikey dog was named "Bibi" and beside him is the pig, each of them about 7cm long. The pig illustrates the brown patches on cream colouring that was popular with many Bimini animal models.

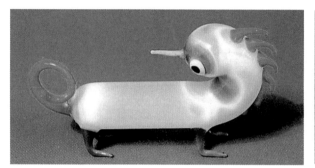 

The two little cats with a rat are part of Pipin Henzl's collection. The red cat was a gift to his wife's elder sister when she was about seven years old, as a reward for visiting the dentist. The two young bulls look ready to fight.

Another very famous Bimini fantasy model is Pegasus, and beside him on the left is the elegant Bimini crane.

Our last two pictures for this chapter are the ass and the camel, both in the Bimini brown on cream colours.

LIST OF ILLUSTRATIONS FOR CHAPTER 4

1: Black horse. Bimini model 741, Neuwirth catalogue 458, height 9.4cm. There is a smaller version, Bimini model 742, Neuwirth catalogue number 459, height 8.5cm. This model was also made in brown on cream.

2: Elephant Bimini model 852, Neuwirth catalogue 525, height 6.6cm, length 10.1cm.

3: Mythical animal – unicorn Bimini model 771, Neuwirth catalogue 480, height 22.2cm.

4: Grasshopper Bimini model 605, Neuwirth catalogue 397, length 5cm. height 2.5cm.

5: Hedgehog Bimini model 791, Neuwirth catalogue 489, height 2.6cm length 4cm.

6: Magpie (corvidae family) Bimini model 611, Neuwirth catalogue 405, height 6.3cm.

7: Owl Bimini model 831, Neuwirth catalogue 519, height 2.6cm.

8: Two Pelicans Bimini model 781, Neuwirth catalogue 483 and 485, height 5.5cm and 7.5cm.

9: Bibi little dog, Bimini model 951, Neuwirth catalogue 576, length 7.2cm.

10: Pig Bimini model 822 (variant), Neuwirth catalogue 515, length 6.7cm.

11: Two cats Bimini model 921, Neuwirth catalogue 554 (white) and 555 (red), height 5cm.

12: Rat Bimini model 911, Neuwirth catalogue 550, length 8.3cm.

13: Young bulls tussling, Bimini model 633, Neuwirth catalogue 414, height 4cm length 6cm.

14: Crane Bimini model 752, Neuwirth catalogue 475, height approx.. 17cm.

15: Pegasus Bimini model 959, Neuwirth catalogue 585, height 19.3cm.

16: Ass Bimini model 744, Neuwirth catalogue 468, height 8.5cm. There is also a "screaming" version of the ass, Bimini model 745 and Neuwirth catalogue 469.

17: Large camel Bimini model 731, Neuwirth catalogue 454, height approx.. 12cm.

5: PERFUME BOTTLES

Bimini made such stunningly beautiful perfume bottles that we have given them a whole chapter. Here is the Bimini perfume bottle containing an angel holding a bird in a cage. The traditional method of making glass items inside a bottle is to enter them through the base and then seal the base seamlessly. However, some of the items in Bimini bottles are larger than the size of the base, making for a complicated delicate operation.

Equally beautiful are the perfume bottles with cupid firing an arrow at a heart on the outside of the bottle. Fritz Lampl said that getting the arrow to point directly at the heart was part of the difficulty of making these.

The same bottle was made with a white cupid, shown here.

Flowers and bouquets were also included inside Bimini perfume bottles, like these two here.

Each of the perfume bottles shown above has an elaborate stopper with a decorated surface. Sometimes the heart was gold coloured and sometimes the little dots on the stoppers were also gold.

There is evidence in the Bimini catalogues that the company also made simple scent bottles without these fancy stoppers, with all kinds of plants and animals inside. Here is a barely legible copy of the page showing these tiny bottles in a Bimini catalogue (Neuwirth pages 316-317). The catalogue page is dated 1938 and headed "Bimini Scent bottles with glass flowers and figures cast inside".

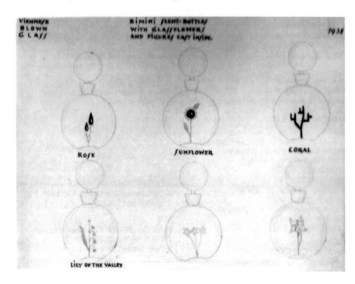

Bimini Glass

The stoppers on these bottles are simple, not decorated. The items listed and shown inside these bottles are a heart, snowman, trefoil, mushroom, gentian, rose, violet, sunflower, coral, cyclamen, lily of the valley, and mistletoe. The accompanying text says the export price per bottle was S 2.80 each for the first six and S 3.20 for the second six. The little scent bottle below may be the Lily of the Valley example. It has a label "Made in Austria" which, according to Neuwirth (page 462) was sometimes used by Bimini.

Bimini made many designs of scent and perfume bottles that did not have inclusions. Here are three of them, on the left is the perfume bottle called "Eros", in the centre is "Damon" and on the right is a little perfume bottle made in London during the Orplid period.

LIST OF ILLUSTRATIONS FOR CHAPTER 5

1: Perfume bottle with angel carrying bird in cage. Listed in Neuwirth catalogue 378

2: Perfume bottle with black cupid,   Neuwirth catalogue 385. Height 9cm

3: Perfume bottle with black cupid, Neuwirth catalogue 385. Height 9cm

4: Perfume bottle with white cupid, Neuwirth catalogue 385. Height 9cm

5: Perfume bottle with white cupid, Neuwirth catalogue 385. Height 9cm

6: Perfume bottle with bouquet inside, Neuwirth catalogue 383. Height 8cm.

7: Perfume bottle with one flower, Neuwirth catalogue 378. Height 9cm

8: Drawings of scent bottles from Bimini catalogue page. Neuwirth catalogue 354.

9: Scent bottle with Lily of the Valley inside, Neuwirth catalogue 359

10: "Eros" perfume bottle, Bimini model 512, Neuwirth catalogue 319, height 11.2cm

11: "Damon" perfume bottle. Bimini model 505. Neuwirth catalogue 311, height 12cm.

11: Orplid perfume bottle made in London by Fritz Lampl. Height approx. 12 cm

6: BUTTONS, BROOCHES AND HATPINS

The Bimini workshop in London made glass buttons from its early days in 1939. This was partly to take advantage of the war-time shortage of good quality buttons in Britain and partly to provide semi-skilled work for Fritz Lampl's Austrian refugee friends who needed employment when they first arrived in London. The buttons were made by pressing molten glass into plaster moulds and then decorating and adding brass backs to them. This was work that was easy to learn and although many refugee employees described it as very boring, it did not restrict them from smoking and chatting about politics or their many artistic interests. The little Bimini workshop helped many famous Austrians make contacts and get established in London, including the potter Lucie Rie, the writer Erich Fried.

Whilst some Bimini buttons were made by semi-skilled refugee employees, the designs produced at Bimini in London were all by Fritz Lampl. Sometimes they were based on ancient coins and medallions from the Victoria and Albert Museum collections. And some items like the delicate little blown glass creations used for necklaces, brooches, bracelets, and hat pins required experienced glass artists like Ellen Turner and Ben George. And Lucie Rie the potter contributed ceramic components. But the designs were all Bimini designs by Fritz Lampl. Here are some examples of Bimini/Orplid pressed glass buttons, which were often gilded or decorated with coloured glass enamel. They measure 3cm across and have the Bimini/Orplid brass back.

Bimini Glass

This was the first time Bimini creations were made permanently identifiable as Fritz Lampl's designs. They had the little flowerpot logo impressed on the brass backs which were attached to these buttons. There were two versions of the Bimini button backs, one stamped MADE IN ENGLAND BIMINI Ltd with the flower pot logo surrounded by a circle and the words BIMINI LIMITED around it. The other one just had MADE IN ENGLAND with the flower pot logo not surrounded by a circle. The first one relates to the period from 1941 to 1948 when Bimini was incorporated as a UK limited company. The second one was used when the name of the company was changed to Orplid Ltd. in 1948 and possibly earlier.

Not all Bimini/Orplid buttons had a brass back. Some, like the ones sewn onto this padded satin display cushion, were made with a glass loop for stitching. This pad would have been used as a salesman's display to show customers the range of button designs available. The pad measures 34cm wide by 20cm and each button is approximately 3cm across.

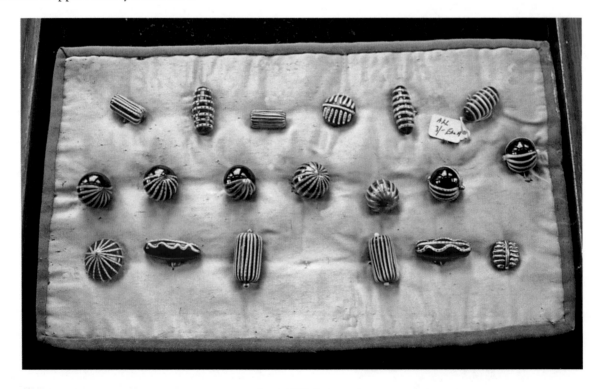

Two of the buttons are shown in more detail below. These were blown glass, not pressed, and they required a skilled glass blower. The Bimini/Orplid workshop in London employed skilled local glass blowers just as they did in Vienna. Ellen Turner and Ben George were two of them.

In addition to making buttons Bimini/Orplid made tiny ornaments to put onto hatpins, several of which are shown below. These were hand blown with lampwork decoration again requiring a skilled glass blower. Hatpins were very popular during and just after the war years. Wearing hats was fashionable and these hatpins were cheerful and decorative at a time when such things were in very short supply in Britain.

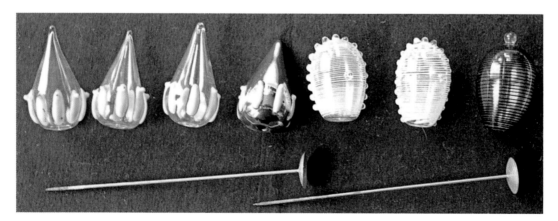

Bimini Glass

The selection below includes blown glass hatpins and buttons and pressed glass scarf rings. The same designs were sometimes made as buttons and as hatpins. The little crown was one of these. The close-up pictures of the little black and white crown button show the simple glass loop for attaching them to a garment.

Here is an example of an Orplid scarf ring, with a classical medallion pressed into its surface before shaping into a ring and gilding. Beside it is another Orplid scarf ring in red and white glass.

Bimini Glass

Components for Bimini buttons and other items were made in ceramics by Lucie Rie whom Lampl helped to start up in London. Lucie, later Dame Lucie, was grateful to Fritz all her long life. Here is a selection of items made by Lucie Rie some for Bimini and some from later in her career.

Costume jewellery made in glass was another successful and popular line for Fritz Lampl's little workshop. This was not a new venture for Bimini. Beautiful glass jewellery had also been made in the Viennese Bimini workshop.

This delightful Orplid bracelet is 22cm long and 4cm wide. All the parts are made from glass except the little metal fastening clasp.

These two little necklaces were made by Bimini Vienna and were exhibited in the 1930s.

This little brooch has a pin at the back to hold it in place and is intended to hold a flower with its stem kept damp.

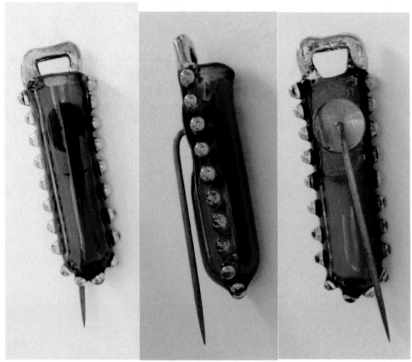

Fantastic sea creatures and birds were designed for brooches and necklaces, blown or crafted in glass and then gilded.

A new logo was designed by Josef Berger in 1948 for the new name Orplid. It was not used on the button backs. It was used on letter headings and invoices, and was accepted and promoted by the fashion press almost seamlessly when Fritz stopped using the name Bimini. Such was his fame that it did not seem to matter. Here is an example of an Orplid button back beside the new Orplid logo.

By 1950 a steady stream of brooches, buttons, hatpins and jewellery were being produced from the Orplid basement workshop in Hampstead, London where Fritz and Hilde lived. Orplid was as much a success as Bimini had been and articles about the firm appeared in Vogue, Design Magazine, the Courier, and many others. In them Lampl was variously described as "The Poet in Glass", "The Wizard in Glass", or in an American publication, "The Talented Briton"! In that austere time, when Britain was recovering from the disastrous costs of the war, glass ornaments seemed both light hearted and appropriate even for the rich to wear. He was selling to the top stores in London and struggling to make output meet demand.

Bimini Glass

With blockades on imports, Orplid had a virtual monopoly of art glassware during the 1940s and early 50s. The collections below are part of Fritz's stock for making up into jewellery.

The costume jewellery produced by Bimini and Orplid included some beautiful little brooches, like these.

Such was Fritz Lampl's fame that he even appeared as the hero of a children's book, "The Mystery of the Pink Elephants" by Mary Maloney, published in 1945. In this story a group of children track down a mysterious reference to pink elephants and find Johann, a Fritz Lampl lookalike, in his workshop, where he demonstrates to them the technique of making pink elephants from glass.

Orplid success continued into the 1950s. But as import restrictions were gradually lifted, cheap and cheerful glass imports from Europe were allowed into Britain. Lampl struggled to compete, Hilde's dress designs were failing in popularity, and their savings were stolen by a trusted office employee. This was too much for Fritz and he died of a heart attack in 1955. Hilde died a few weeks later and there was no-one to take over. The glory that had been Bimini Glass died with him, leaving only the beautiful legacy of his glass.

List of Illustrations for Chapter 6

Note: When the company name was changed from Bimini to Orplid the same production carried on in a new venue and the words on the brass button backs were changed.

1: A selection of Bimini/Orplid pressed glass buttons 3cm wide for fitting with brass backs.

2: Brass button backs for Bimini (left) and Orplid (right).

3: Display pad with hand blown Bimini/Orplid buttons sewn on, each 3cm wide, pad 34 x 20cm.

4: Red blown glass button with white and gold decoration, 3cm wide.

5: Blue blown glass button with white stripes and gold dots, 3cm wide.

6: Collection of hand blown and decorated hat pin tops for fitting to the pins shown.

7: Selection of Bimini/Orplid blown glass buttons and hatpin tops.

8 and 9: Close-up of Bimini/Orplid black crown button, blown glass with white decoration, showing glass loop for sewing.

10 and 11: Bimini/Orplid pressed and hand manipulated glass scarf ring with gilded medallion.

12: Hand manipulated Bimini/Orplid scarf ring in red and clear striped glass.

13: Collection of ceramic components by Lucie Rie for Bimini/Orplid costume jewelry and buttons.

14: Bimini glass bracelet from the London period entirely made from glass except for the tiny metal fastening clasp. Length 21cm width 3cm

15 and 16: Two small Bimini necklaces from the Viennese period, exhibited in the 1930s.

17: Amber blown glass brooch for holding a flower with its stem kept damp inside the tube, 6cm long.

18: Collection of Bimini/Orplid brooches and jewelry.

19: An Orplid button back and the Orplid logo designed by Josef Berger in 1948.

20 and 21: Two boxes of Orplid jewelry parts.

22: Bimini/Orplid glass brooches with gilt decoration.

23: Bimini/Orplid glass brooches and necklace.

Appendix

More Photographs from the Bimini Story

Sketch of a London scene by Fritz Lampl signed F Lampl 51.

Sketch of a scene in a London park by Fritz Lampl.

Fritz Lampl's registration certificate for the National Register of Industrial Art Designers in November 1938.

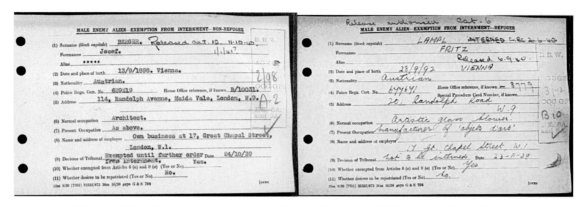

Enemy Alien Internment notices for Joseph Berger and Fritz Lampl in 1939.

Below: A page from a Bimini catalogue of designs.

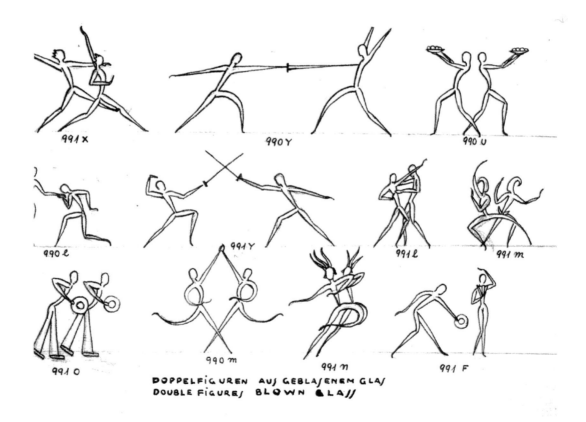

Georg Karpeles-Schenker, the Playboy of Vienna, photographed in 1924 when he was 21.

Fritzi Berger dress design from Wiener Werkstatte postcard in the 1920s.

A painting by Margarete Hamerschlag of her son Raymond Berger holding his gas mask during the war (private collection).

Another war-time painting by Margarete Hamerschlag showing a London barrage balloon over this small island in the Grand Union Canal in an area known as Little Venice, Paddington. The two half-sunk barges lay derelict throughout the war, but today the area is popular for its luxury restaurants, affluent dwellings and up-market house-boats.

This letter heading from 1942 of the Craftworkers Association Edinburgh proudly announced that they were "Agents for Bimini Products" giving an indication of the prestige attached to Bimini at this time.

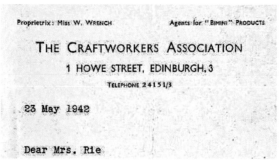

Two of Hilde Lampl's dress designs from War time London. By then the flamboyance of Viennese days was not fashionable in haute couture, being replaced by simplicity and austerity. Hilde enhanced her designs with beautiful buttons and trimmings.

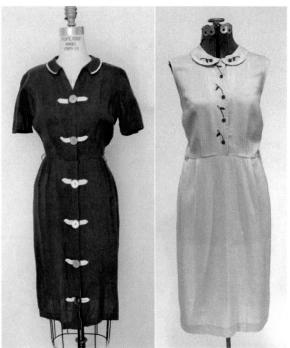

The Orplid logo was designed by Josef Berger c. 1948. It was used on letter headings and invoices, but not on glass labels nor on button backs.

Orplid Glass Ltd certificate of invitation to display their glass at the Festival of Britain in 1951.

Raymond Berger is also an artist. After working in the TV industry and Lecturing at Art College, he now works in Fine Art. His painting Maze, which is in acrylic paint with collage, was hung in the Royal West of England Academy show recently.

A small garden party held at Fritz and Hilde Lampl's house in Hampstead, London in 1939.

A cartoon by the famous Viennese cartoonist Peter Eng, showing Fritz Lampl in his Bimini studio in Vienna blowing a glass animal and asking "What should I blow next?" His customer, a Viennese painter, suggests "Blow the Radetzky March".

List of Illustrations in the Appendix

1: Small Fritz Lampl sketch of a London scene signed F Lampl 51.

2: Small Fritz Lampl sketch of a scene in a London park.

3: Certificate from the National Register of Industrial Art Designers in November 1938 for Fritz Lampl.

4: Internment of Enemy Aliens notices for Joseph Berger and Fritz Lampl in 1939.

5: A page from a Bimini catalogue showing figurine designs.

6: Drawing from Bimini catalog showing a sportsman and girl playing a flute.

7: Photograph of Georg Karpeles-Schenker, the Playboy of Vienna, in 1924 when he was 21.

8: Dress design by Fritzi Berger shown on a Wiener Werkstatte postcard.

9: Painting by Margarete Hamerschlag of her son Raymond Berger holding his gas mask during the war

10: War-time painting by Margarete Hamerschlag showing Little Venice area, Paddington.

11: Letter heading from 1942, Craftworkers Association Edinburgh "Agents for Bimini Products".

12: Two of Hilde Lampl's dress designs from War time London.

13: The Orplid logo designed by Josef Berger c. 1948.

14: Orplid Glass Ltd certificate of invitation to display their glass at the Festival of Britain in 1951.

15: "Maze" an acrylic painting with collage by Raymond Berger.

16: Photograph of a small garden party at Fritz and Hilde Lampl's house in Hampstead, London 1939.

17: Cartoon by Viennese cartoonist Peter Eng, of Fritz Lampl in his Viennese Bimini studio.

References and Further Reading

- Arwas, Victor: *Glass Art Nouveau to Art Deco,* published by Academy Editions, 1987
- Adrian, Carole: *The Poet, the Architect and the Playboy* article in The National Button Bulletin, February 2011.
- Berger, Raymond: *Bimini and Orplid Glass, the Internet, and Me* article in The Glass Cone issue 58, 2001.
- Berger, Raymond and Bowey, Angela: *Bimini and Orplid Glass* article on the Glass Museum website 2003. http://www.theglassmuseum.com/bimini.htm
- Berger, Josef, FRIBA: *The Poet in Glass, Fritz Lampl* unpublished manuscript written c. 1988.
- Berger, Raymond: *Bimini and Orplid Glass, the Internet, and Me,* published in The Glass Cone, issue 58, 2001.
- Berger, Raymond: *Orplid Glass 1940-1955* article in The Glass Cone issue 41, 1996.
- Berger, Raymond: *Bimini and the Nude Lady Cocktail Sets,* article in The Glass Cone Winter 2015.
- Berger Raymond with Angela Bowey: *Bimini and Orplid Glass* 2003, the Glass Museum On Line.
- Berger-Hamerschlag, Margarete: *Journey Into a Fog,* published by Victor Gollancz, London 1955.
- Berger-Hamerschlag, Margarete: *Die Stadt* (ten woodcuts) Vienna 1923.
- Berger-Hamerschlag, Margarete: *Kinderfreuden* (text and woodcut illustrations)Vienna 1921
- Birks, Tony: *Lucie Rie,* Stenlake Publishing Ltd, revised edition 2009.
- Blau, Eve: *The Architecture of Red Vienna. 1919-1934.,* The MIT Press, 1999
- Bowey, Angela: *Pirelli Glass,* OAR Publishing New Zealand, 2016.
- Bowey, Angela with Bob Martin, Christine Burley and Raymond Berger: *London Lampworkers: Pirelli, Bimini and Komaromy Glass* , published by OAR Publishing 2013.
- Bowey, Angela: *Bimini Glass: A short explanation* in the Glass Encyclopedia on line: http://www.glassencyclopedia.com/Biminiglass.html   2008.
- Chappell, Connery: *Island of Barbed Wire - Internment on the Isle of Man in WWII,* Crowood Press Ltd, 1984
- Couper, Emmanuel (ed) *The Life and Work of Lucie Rie 1902-1995,* Ceramic Review Publishing Ltd, 2002.
- *Directory for the British Glass Industry* in the Annual Reports of the Society of Glass Technology.
- Grace's Guide *Bimini of 10 Mount Row.* https://www.gracesguide.co.uk/Bimini (accessed 2018)
- Gruber, Helmut: *Red Vienna. Experiment in Working Class Culture, 1919-1934.,* Oxford Uni, Press, 1991
- Gunther, John (1933). *Inside Europe* (7th, 1940 ed.). New York: Harper & Brothers. p. 379.
- Hajdamach, Charles: *20th Century British Glass,* pages 178-180; Antique Collectors Club, 2009.
- Hamerschlag, Margarete: See Berger-Hamerschlag, Margarete.
- Haanstra, Ivo: *Glass Fact File a-z* published by Millers, 2001.
- Hartmann, Carolus: *Glasmarken Lexicon 1600-1945* published by Arnoldsche Art Publishers, 1999
- Heath, Sophie *The Lucie Rie archive at the Crafts Study Centre.* https://vads.ac.uk/learning/csc/rie/essay.html
- Janik, Allan and Toulmin, Stephen: *Wittgenstein's Vienna.* Simon & Schuster, New York 1973
- Malonoey, Mary:*The Mystery of the Pink Elephants* - an account of lampworking in a children's story, based on Fritz Lampl. Published by Oxford Univsity Press, 1945.
- Neuwirth, Dr Waltraud: *Bimini - Wiener Glaskunst des Art Deco. (Bimini - Viennese Art Deco Art Glass),* published by Neuwirth, 1992. The author is an eminent Austrian Design Historian, and her book followed a major exhibition of Bimini in 1992 in Austria.
- Neuwirth, Waltraud: *Die Bimini-Werkstatt* published in Antiquitaten-Zeitung 25, in 1980.

- Passauer Glasmuseum (ed) *Das Bohmische Glas 1700-1950: Band VI Art Deco to Moderne* chapter *Bimini-Werkstatte Wien*
- Pina, Leslie: *circa Fifties Glass from Europe and America* published by Schiffer, 1997.
- Pholz, Veronika: *A clan of artists in exile. From Austria to Britain* chapter three in *Exile and Patronage: Cross cultural negotiations beyond the Third Rrich,* by Andrew Chandler, Katarzyna Stocklosa, Jutta Vinzent (eds), published by Transaction Publishers (USA and UK), 2006.
- Poe, Edgar Allan: *Die Maske des roten Todes*, with woodcuts by Margarete Berger, Vienna 1924
- Polanyi, Karl (2001) [1944]. *The Great Transformation*. Boston: Beacon Press. p. 298.
- Pottery and Glass Trades Gazette Reference Book and Directory 1949, page 43 [29x]
- Truitt, Robert and Deborah: *Bohemian Glass 1915 - 1945 Volume 2,* 1998, page 118.
- Zweig, Stefan, autobiography *The World of Yesterday: Memories of a European* Stockholm, 1942; English version - Viking Press, 1943. Reprinted 2013 by University of Nebraska Press.
- Zweig, Stefan with illustrations by Margarete Hamerschlag: *The Buried Candelabrum,* London 1937.

Fritz Lampl with his glass cabinet about 1950.

INDEX

Fritz Lampl in 1931

Bimini Glass

Other Books on Glass by Angela Bowey.

Available from Amazon (search Angela Bowey) or see www.glass-time.com

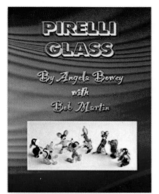

Pirelli Glass offers a definitive guide to identify and learn more about Pirelli Glass including the people who worked there and the history of the company and its products. How did Pirelli came to work so closely with the Scottish paperweight makers Vasart, and the range of Pirelli/Vasart products. Chapters 3 to 6 show all the known Pirelli glass models from company catalogues, the Disney cartoon figures and commissions for the Guinness Company, plus those known from Pirelli advertisements, from Pirelli labels, or confirmed by the glass artists who made them (Bob Martin and Mick Munns). If you are a collector or a trader in this kind of glass, invest in this book – you will enjoy it!

.

New Zealand Glass includes many original catalogue pictures and dozens of photographs. This is the expanded 2nd Edition of this comprehensive guide to understanding and identifying New Zealand Glass. New in the 2nd Edition - an expanded section on the glassware made by Crown Crystal Glass in Australia in the years before New Zealand had its own glass factory. If you are a collector of New Zealand Glass or a Trader in Glass, you need the information offered here. It is a really useful book for identifying New Zealand Glass.

London Lampworkers is the first in a trilogy on Pirelli, Bimini and Komaromy Glass. What figurines and other glass did these London Lampworkers really make; how can you identify a genuine piece; and is yours worth hundreds or is it just a ten dollar copy? This short introductory book will help you identify Pirelli, Bimini and Komaromy glass as well as introduce the people who made it. What is it about Pirelli, Bimini and Komaromy that makes them stand out from other lampworkers of the mid 20th century? What is lampworking, who made it and what is its history?

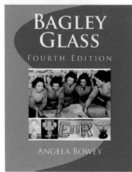

Bagley Glass is the fourth edition of this book about one of the most prolific English makers of art deco pressed glass from the 1920s until 1975. It has hundreds of pictures to help you identify Bagley glass. Who were the Bagleys, where was Bagley's Crystal Glass Company, what did they make and when did they make it? Did Bagley make your piece of glass? Whether its a vase or a bowl, a jug, a plate, or a boudoir set, there's a section that shows the patterns Bagley made with all the patent numbers registered by Bagley. This is a really useful book for identifying Bagley patterns and items.